Contents

A **pull-out answers section** (pages A1 to A8) appears in the centre of this book, between pages 20 and 21. It also gives simple guidance on how best to use this book. Remove this section before you begin working through the tests.

Which picture on the right belongs to the group on the left? Circle the letter.

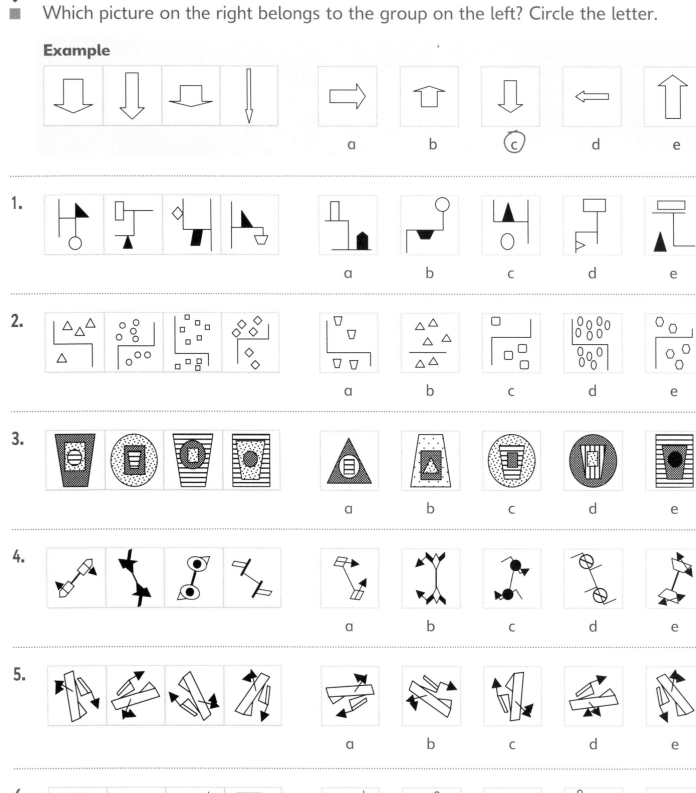

Example

a　　b　　c　　d　　e

1.

a　　b　　c　　d　　e

2.

a　　b　　c　　d　　e

3.

a　　b　　c　　d　　e

4.

a　　b　　c　　d　　e

5.

a　　b　　c　　d　　e

6.

a　　b　　c　　d　　e

Now go on to the next page. ➡

Which of the five pictures on the right goes with the third one to make a pair like the two on the left? Circle the letter.

Example

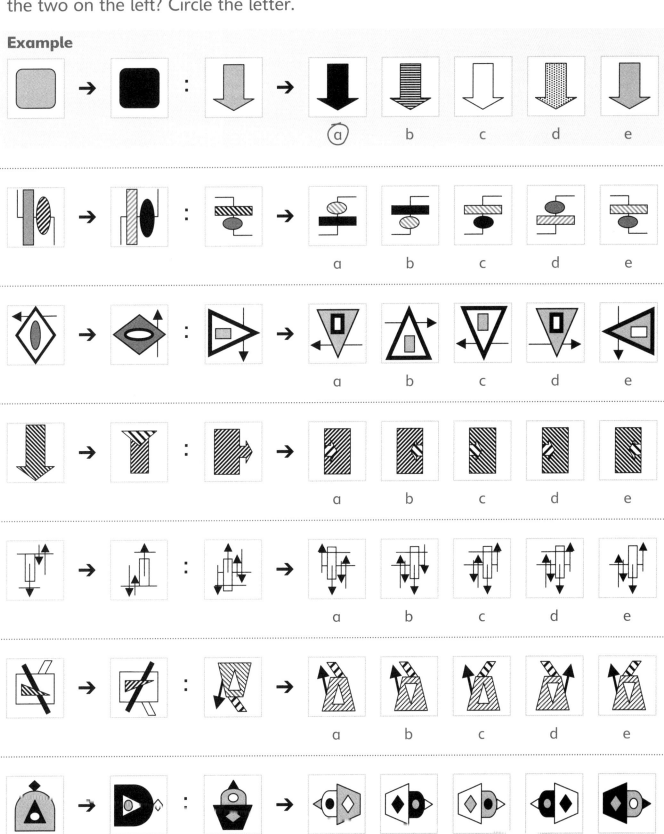

7.

8.

9.

0.

1.

2.

End of test.

| Score: | | Time taken: | | Target met? | |

Which picture on the right goes in the empty space? Circle the letter.

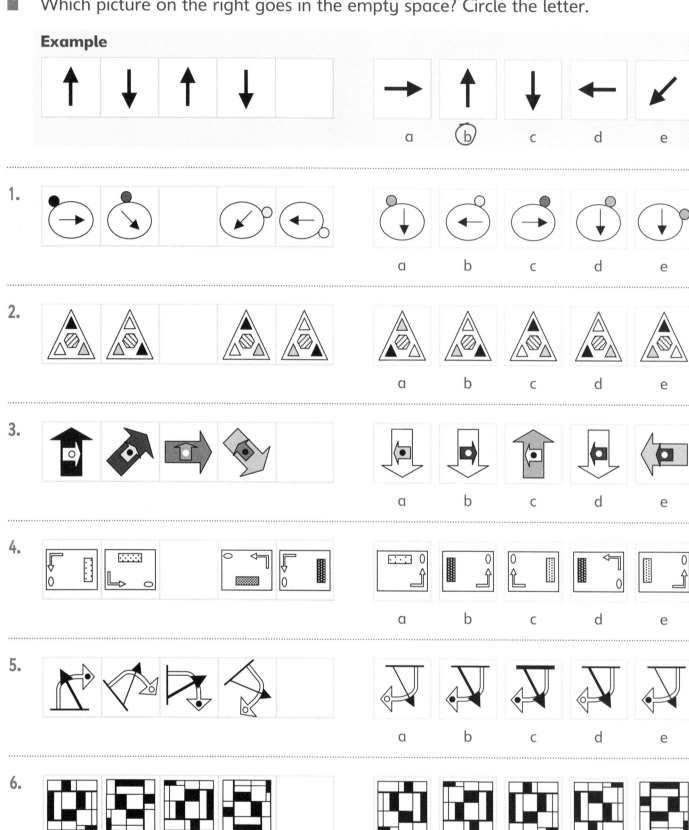

Example

1.

2.

3.

4.

5.

6.

Now go on to the next page. ➡

■ Which picture on the right best fits into the space in the grid? Circle the letter.

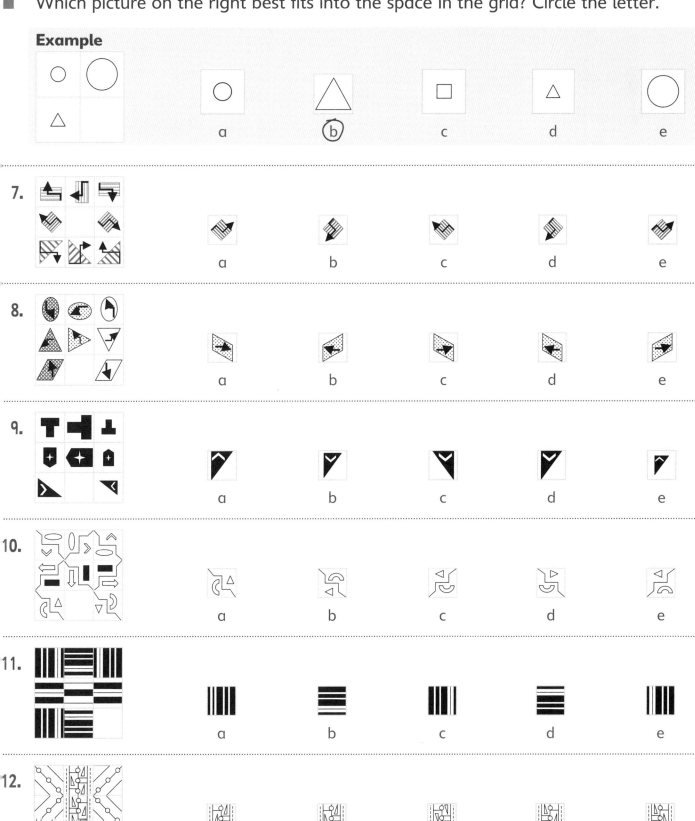

Example

a   b   c   d   e

7.

a   b   c   d   e

8.

a   b   c   d   e

9.

a   b   c   d   e

10.

a   b   c   d   e

11.

a   b   c   d   e

12.

a   b   c   d   e

End of test.

| Score: | | Time taken: | | Target met? | |

In which picture on the right is the picture on the left hidden? Circle the letter.

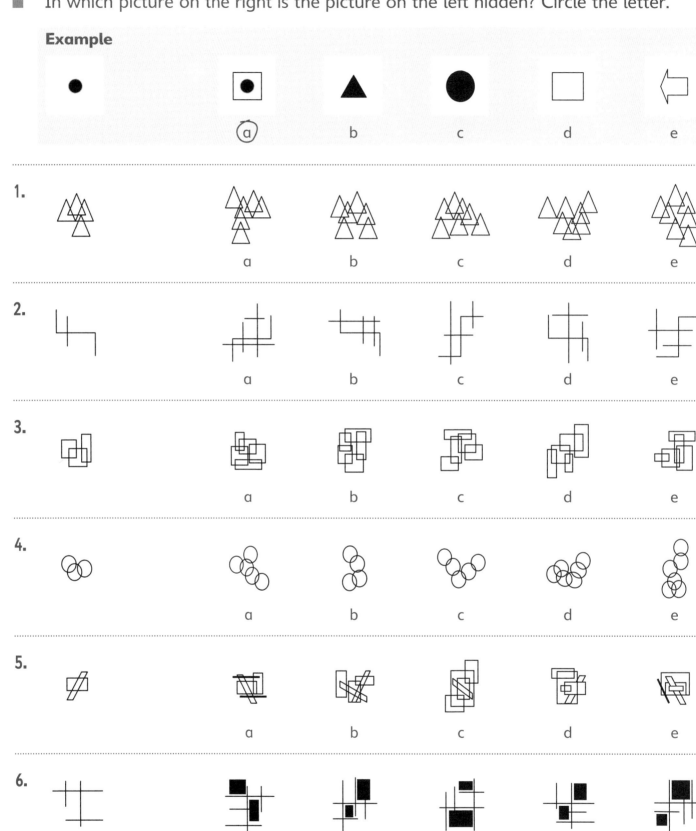

Example

Now go on to the next page.

◼ Which picture is the odd one out? Circle the letter.

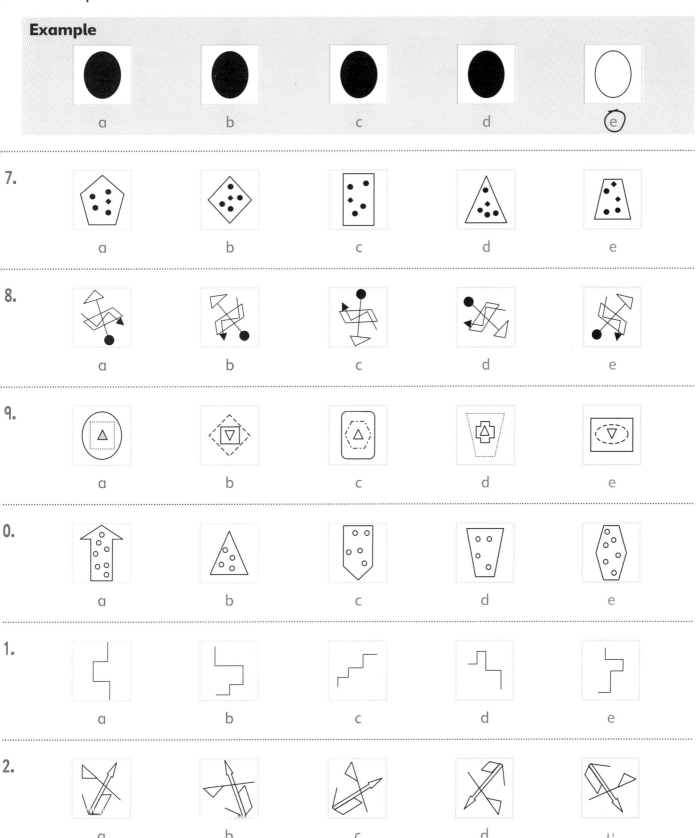

Example

| a | b | c | d | e |

7.

| a | b | c | d | e |

8.

| a | b | c | d | e |

9.

| a | b | c | d | e |

0.

| a | b | c | d | e |

1.

| a | b | c | d | e |

2.

| a | b | c | d | e |

End of test.

| Score: | Time taken: | Target met? |

Which picture on the right is a reflection of the picture on the left? Circle the letter

Example

a   b   c   d   (e)

1.

a   b   c   d   e

2.

a   b   c   d   e

3.

a   b   c   d   e

4.

a   b   c   d   e

5.

a   b   c   d   e

6.

a   b   c   d   e

Now go on to the next page. ➡

■ What is the code of the final picture? Circle the letter.

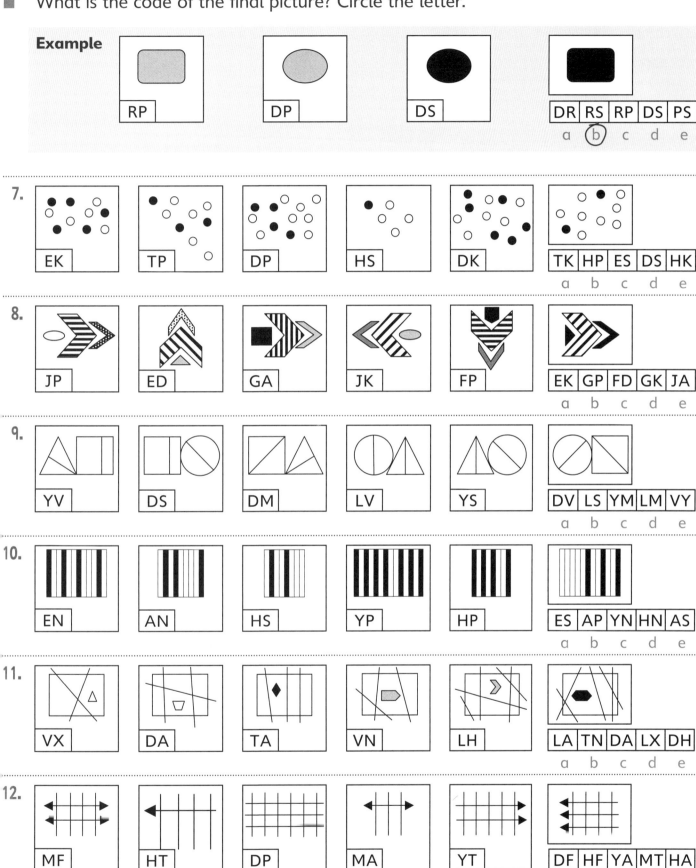

Example

RP	DP	DS	DR RS RP DS PS
			a ⓑ c d e

7.

EK	TP	DP	HS	DK	TK HP ES DS HK
					a b c d e

8.

JP	ED	GA	JK	FP	EK GP FD GK JA
					a b c d e

9.

YV	DS	DM	LV	YS	DV LS YM LM VY
					a b c d e

10.

EN	AN	HS	YP	HP	ES AP YN HN AS
					a b c d e

11.

VX	DA	TA	VN	LH	LA TN DA LX DH
					a b c d e

12.

MF	HT	DP	MA	YT	DF HF YA MT HA
					a b c d e

End of test.

Score:	Time taken:	Target met?

⬇
■ Which picture on the right can be made by combining the first two shapes? Circle the letter.

Example

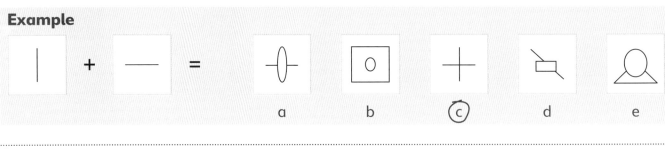

a   b   c   d   e

1.
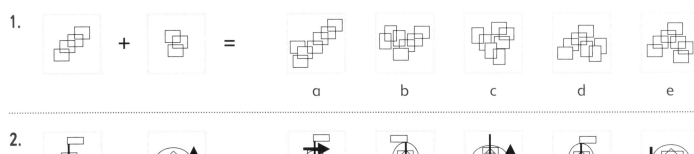

a   b   c   d   e

2.
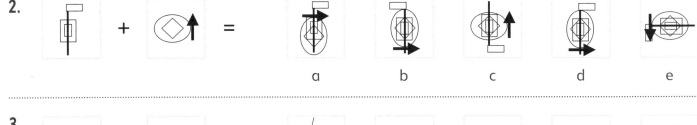

a   b   c   d   e

3.
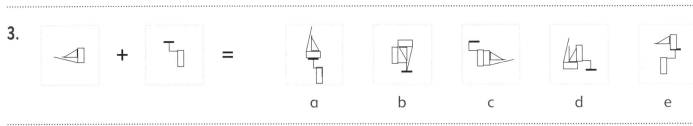

a   b   c   d   e

4.
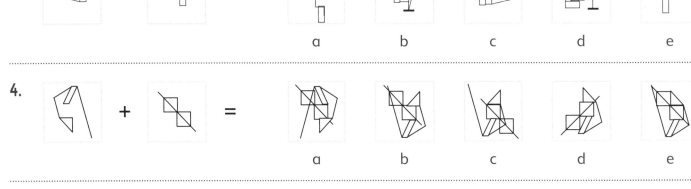

a   b   c   d   e

5.
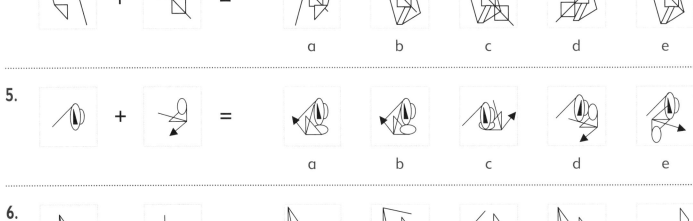

a   b   c   d   e

6.
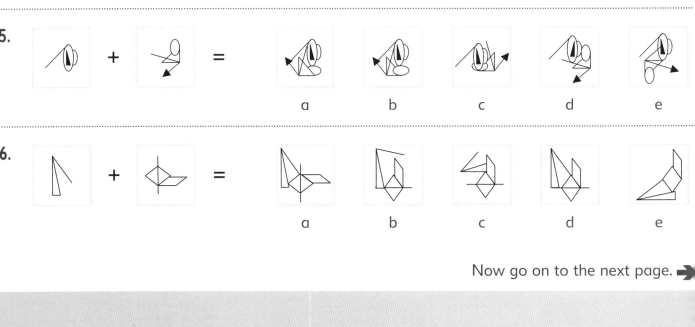

a   b   c   d   e

Now go on to the next page. ➡

■ Which cube can be made exactly from the net? Circle the letter.

Example

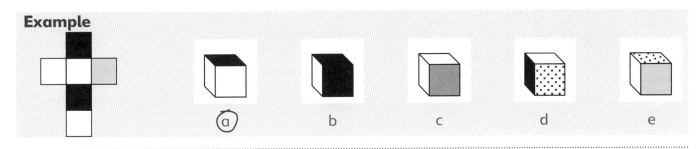

aⓑ b c d e

7.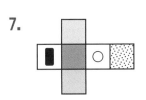

   a b c d e

8.

   a b c d e

9.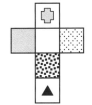

   a b c d e

10.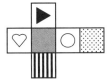

   a b c d e

11.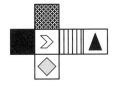

   a b c d e

12.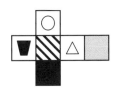

   a b c d e

End of test.

Score:		Time taken:		Target met?	

Which picture on the right goes in the empty space? Circle the letter.

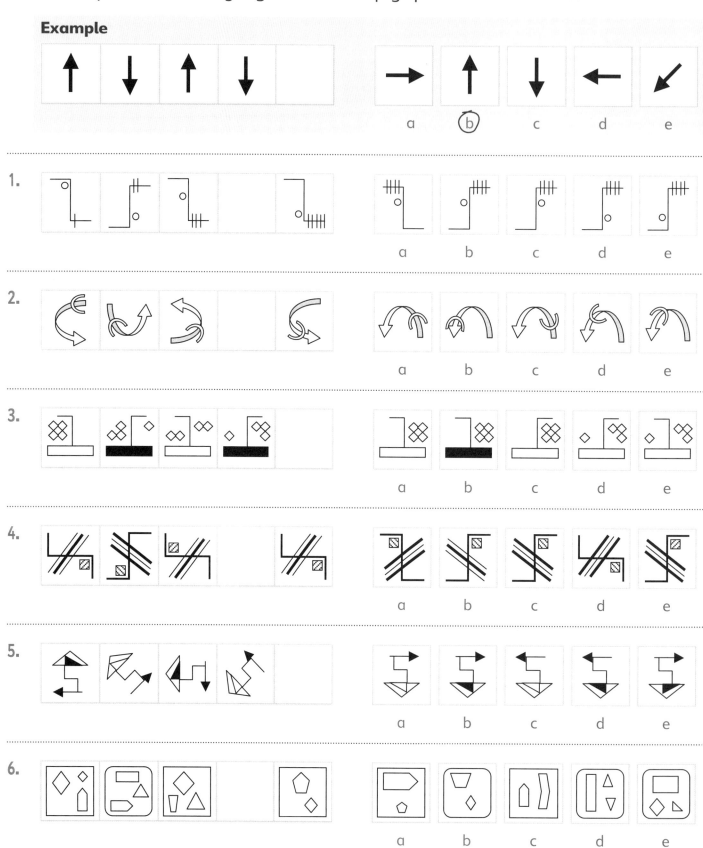

Example

a   b   c   d   e

1.

a   b   c   d   e

2.

a   b   c   d   e

3.

a   b   c   d   e

4.

a   b   c   d   e

5.

a   b   c   d   e

6.

a   b   c   d   e

Now go on to the next page. ➡

Which picture on the right is a reflection of the picture on the left? Circle the letter.

Example

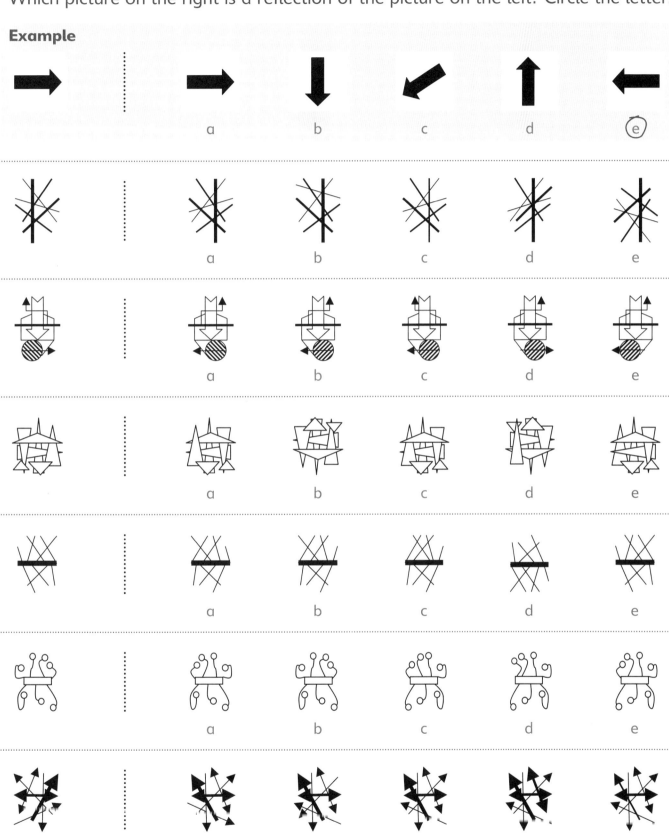

Which of the five pictures on the right goes with the third one to make a pair like the two on the left? Circle the letter.

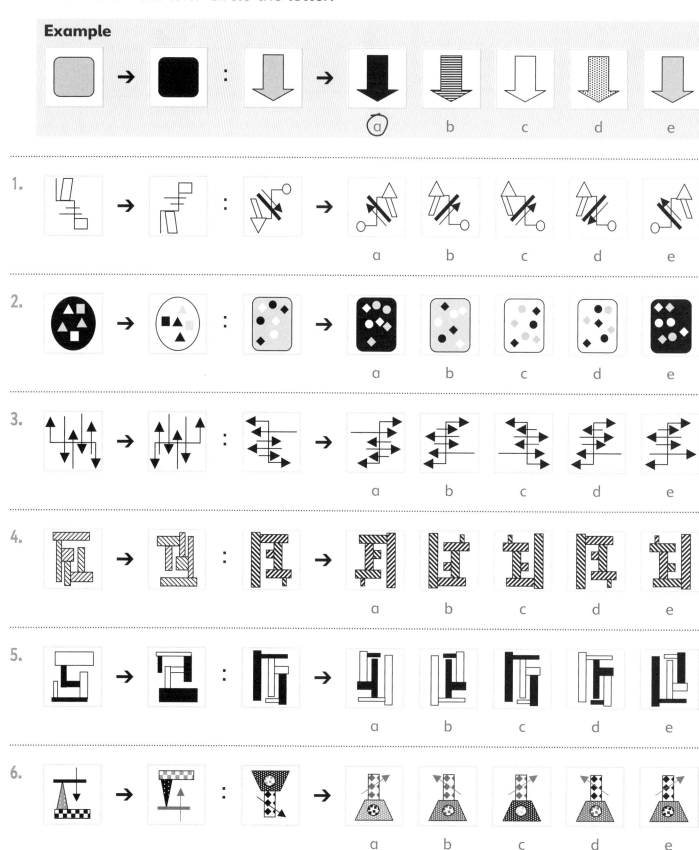

Example

1.

2.

3.

4.

5.

6.

Now go on to the next page.

■ Which picture is the odd one out? Circle the letter.

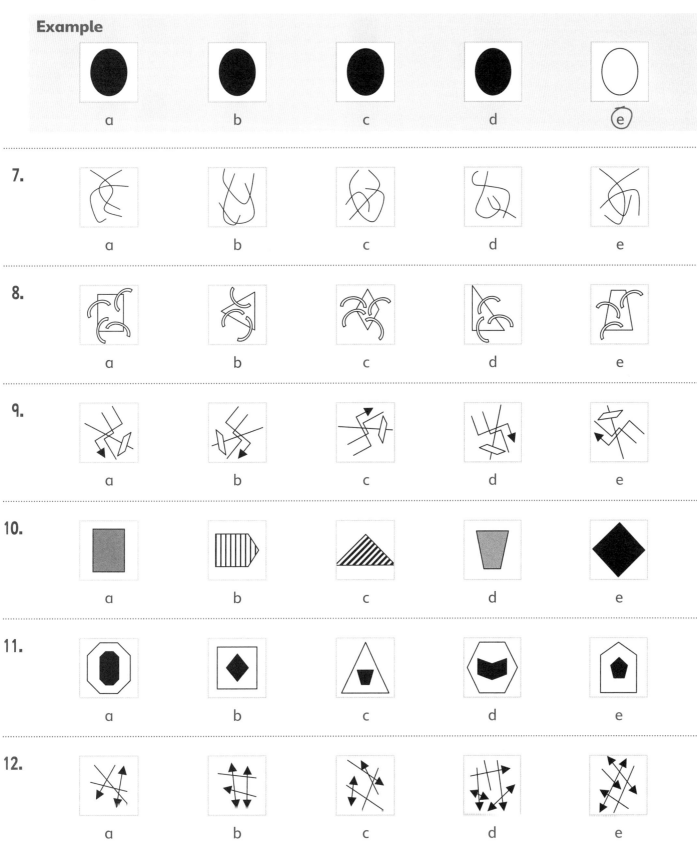

Example

| a | b | c | d | (e) |

7. | a | b | c | d | e |

8. | a | b | c | d | e |

9. | a | b | c | d | e |

10. | a | b | c | d | e |

11. | a | b | c | d | e |

12. | a | b | c | d | e |

End of test.

| Score: | Time taken: | Target met? |

Section 2 Test 2

Which net can be made exactly from the cube? Circle the letter.

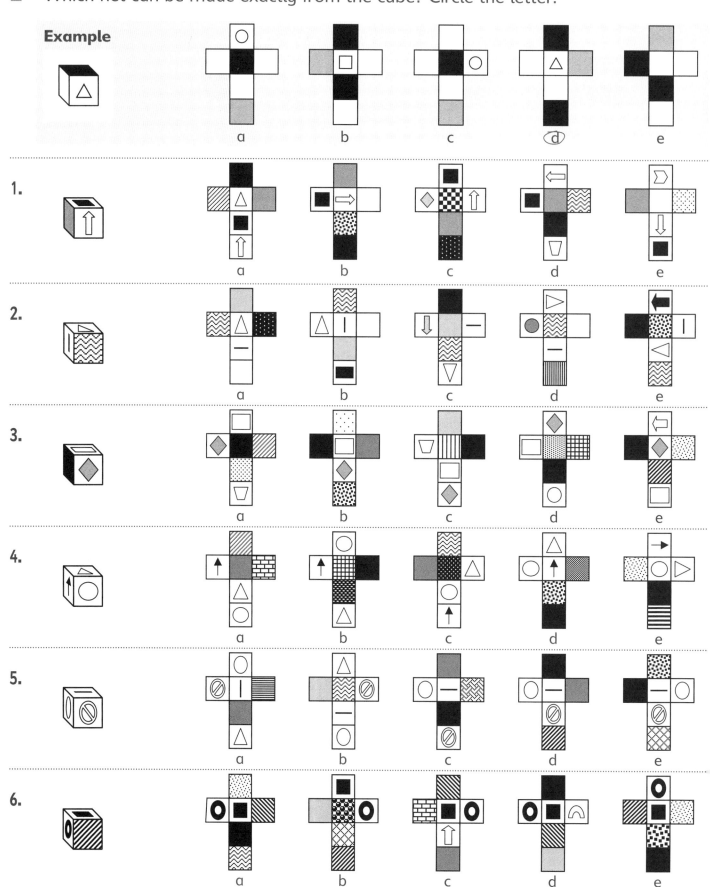

Example

a   b   c   d   e

1.

a   b   c   d   e

2.

a   b   c   d   e

3.

a   b   c   d   e

4.

a   b   c   d   e

5.

a   b   c   d   e

6.

a   b   c   d   e

Now go on to the next page.

In which picture on the right is the picture on the left hidden? Circle the letter.

Example

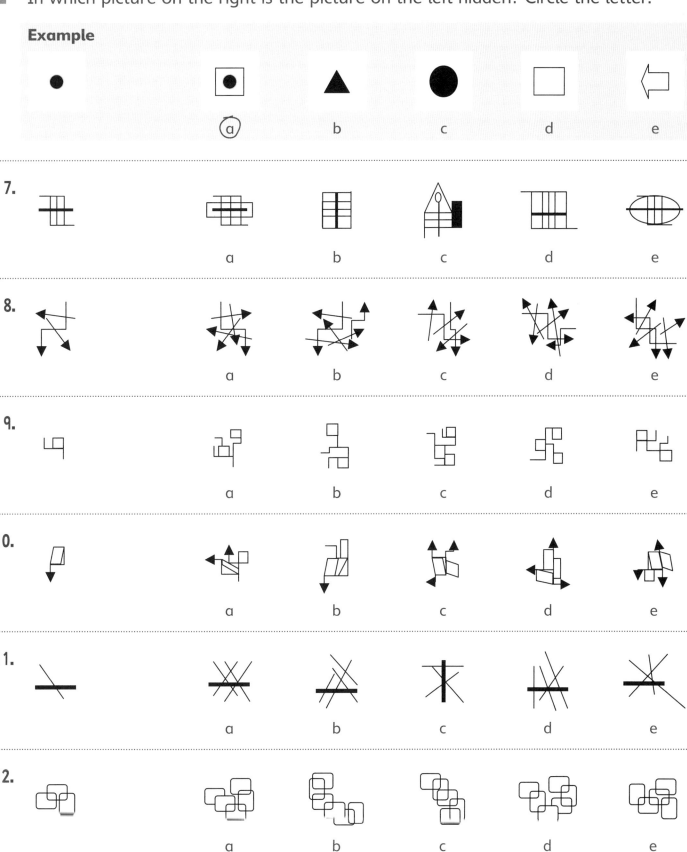

End of test.

| Score: | | Time taken: | | Target met? | |

Which picture on the right best fits into the space in the grid? Circle the letter.

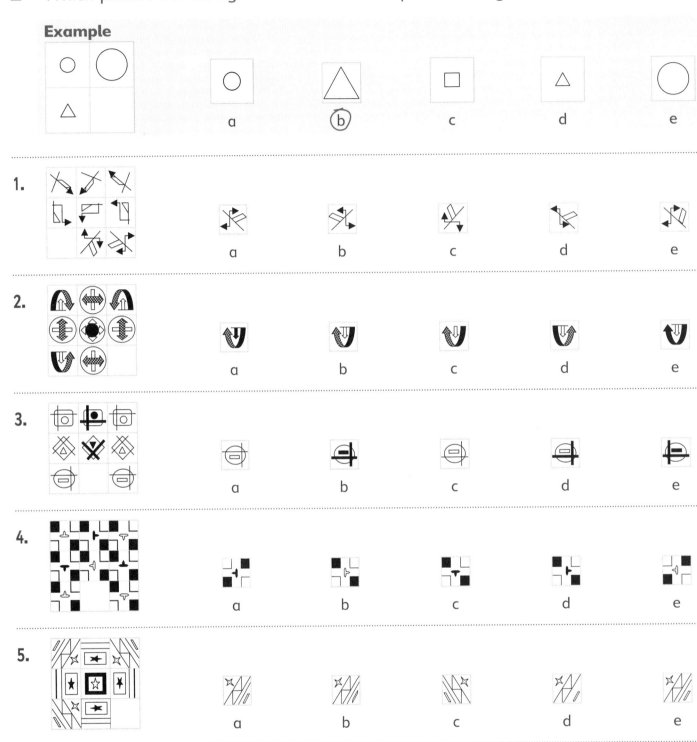

Example

Now go on to the next page. ➔

Non-verbal Reasoning 6 Answers

Notes for parents, tutors, teachers and other adult helpers

- **Non-verbal Reasoning 6** is designed for 11- and 12-year-olds, but may also be suitable for some children of other ages.

- Remove this pull-out section before giving the book to the child.

- Before the child begins work on the first test, read together the instructions on page 2, headed **Introduction**. As you do so, look together at **Section 1 Test 1** and point out to the child the different elements.

- Make sure that the child understands how to answer multiple choice questions and that he or she has a pencil and eraser. You should also ensure that the child is able to see a clock or a watch.

- Explain to the child how he or she should go about timing the test. Alternatively, you may wish to time the test yourself. When the child has finished the test, one of you should complete the **Time taken** box, which appears at the end of the test.

- Mark the child's work using this pull-out section, giving one mark for each correct answer. Then complete the **Score** box at the end of the test.

- The table below shows you how to mark the **Target met?** box and the **Action** notes give you some guidance as you plan the next step. However, these are suggestions only. Please use your own judgement as you decide how best to proceed.

- Whatever the child's score, always encourage the child to have another go at the questions that he or she got wrong without looking at the solutions. If the child's answers are still incorrect, work through these questions together. Demonstrate the correct method if necessary.

Score	Time taken	Target met?	Action
1–6	Any	No	Give the child the previous book in the series. Provide help and support as needed.
7–9	Any	No	Encourage the child to keep practising using the tests in this book. The child may need to repeat some tests. If so, wait a few weeks or the child may simply remember the correct answers. Provide help and support as needed.
10–12	Over target – child took too long	No	
10–12	On target – child took suggested time or less	Yes	Encourage the child to keep practising using further tests in this book.

The **Understanding Reasoning** series, also available from Schofield & Sims, provides clear explanations on how to answer reasoning questions. It also provides 'Tips for tests' and 'Tips for revision'. For further details on this and other series that help children and young people to prepare for school selection tests, and for free downloads relating to the **Rapid Reasoning Tests**, visit www.schofieldandsims.co.uk

Answers

Section 1 Test 1 (pages 4–5)

1. **a** Each picture contains a line and an angled line placed part way along the straight line, plus a black shape and a white shape that both touch the lines.
2. **d** Each picture contains two more shapes above an angled line than below it.
3. **c** Each picture contains the same three types of shading.
4. **d** Each picture contains the same shape at either end but with a 180° rotation.
5. **a** Each picture contains a rotation of the same shape.
6. **b** Each picture contains an arrow, pointing to a circle, which crosses either the rectangle or the line.
7. **b** The angled line is reflected in the vertical mirror line, the striped shape becomes black and the grey shape becomes striped.
8. **a** The picture rotates 90° clockwise, and the colour and the outline of the shapes swap.
9. **d** The arrow head slides to the opposite side of the rectangle and its stripes get thicker, while the stripes in the rectangle are reflected.
10. **d** The picture rotates 180°.
11. **e** The picture is reflected in the horizontal mirror line.
12. **b** The picture rotates 90° clockwise, then grey changes to black, black to white, and white to grey.

Section 1 Test 2 (pages 6–7)

1. **d** The small circle moves clockwise around the oval and gets paler, while the arrow rotates 45° clockwise.
2. **a** The colours move clockwise around the internal triangles and the stripes alternate direction in the hexagon.
3. **d** The external arrow rotates 45° clockwise and gets paler, the internal arrow rotates 45° anticlockwise and gets darker, and the inner circle alternates colour.

4. **e** The shapes move anticlockwise inside the large rectangle and the spots in the small inner rectangle get more dense.
5. **b** The picture rotates 45° clockwise, the circle alternates colour, and the arrow alternates thickness while the straight line stays the same thickness.
6. **c** The picture rotates 90° clockwise.
7. **d** The picture rotates 90° anticlockwise.
8. **c** The picture rotates 90° clockwise and gets paler.
9. **d** The picture rotates 90° clockwise and the largest one is in the central column.
10. **c** The picture rotates 90° anticlockwise.
11. **e** The corners are reflected.
12. **b** Each row in the central column is a reflection in the vertical mirror line of the one above.

Section 1 Test 3 (pages 8–9)

1. **c**
2. **e**
3. **a**
4. **d**
5. **b**
6. **c**
7. **e** The others all have four circles and one rhombus.
8. **b** The others are all rotations of the same picture.
9. **a** The others all have a white triangle.
10. **b** The others all have the same number of small circles as there are sides of the large shape.
11. **a** The others all have five right angles and six lines.
12. **d** The others are all rotations of the same shape.

Section 1 Test 4 (pages 10–11)

1. **d**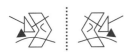

2. **c** (note overlaps)

3. **e**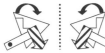

4. **b**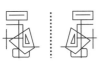

5. **a**   (note overlaps)

6. **e**

7. **c** First letter – number of circles
Second letter – ratio of black to white

8. **a** First letter – small non-arrow shape
Second letter – stripe direction

9. **b** First letter – left shape
Second letter – right shape line direction

10. **a** First letter – number of stripes
Second letter – fraction of stripes shaded

11. **e** First letter – number of line crosses
Second letter – number of sides of
internal shape

12. **b** First letter – type of horizontal line/arrow
Second letter – number of vertical lines

Section 1 Test 5 (pages 12–13)

1. **e**

2. **d**

3. **b**

4. **e**

5. **b**

6. **d**

If in doubt about the nets of cubes, copy them
onto a piece of paper and fold them up.

7. **c**   10. **c**
8. **b**   11. **a**
9. **b**   12. **a**

Section 1 Test 6 (pages 14–15)

1. **c** The angled line alternates direction, the
vertical lines increase by one, and the
circle moves towards the vertical lines
while alternating sides.

2. **e** The arrow rotates 90° anticlockwise,
while the arc moves towards the head of
the arrow and alternates direction.

3. **a** One rhombus at a time moves to the
other side of the line, the rectangle
colour alternates and the position of the
horizontal line at the top alternates.

4. **c** This is a repeating pattern, except for the
striped square which moves corners.

5. **b** This is a repeating pattern with alternate
images that rotate 90° anticlockwise.

6. **d** The number of sides of the internal
shapes reduces by one each time while
the large outer shape alternates.

7. **a** (note line thickness)

8. **b**

9. **c**

Answers

10. b [figure]

11. e [figure]

12. c [figure]

Section 2 Test 1 (pages 16–17)

1. **b** The picture is reflected in the horizontal mirror line.
2. **e** The colours change: black to white, grey to black, white to grey.
3. **a** The picture is reflected in the vertical mirror line.
4. **e** The picture is rotated 180° and the stripes are reflected.
5. **b** The picture is reflected in the horizontal mirror line and the colours swap.
6. **a** The picture is reflected in the horizontal mirror line and the grey and black swap.
7. **d** The others all have lines that cross in four places.
8. **e** The others all have the same number of arcs as sides of shape.
9. **a** The others are all rotations of the same shape but **a** is a reflection.
10. **d** The others all have right angles.
11. **c** The internal and external shapes in the others have the same number of sides.
12. **b** The others all have five points where the lines and arrows cross.

Section 2 Test 2 (pages 18–19)

If in doubt about the nets of cubes, copy them onto a piece of paper and fold them up.

1. **d**   4. **e**
2. **c**   5. **a**
3. **b**   6. **b**
7. **b** [figure]

8. **d**

9. c [figure]

10. d [figure]

11. a [figure]

12. e [figure]

Section 2 Test 3 (pages 20–21)

1. **a** The picture is rotated 90° clockwise across the row.
2. **b** Reflective corners
3. **b** Across the row the picture is reflected in the horizontal mirror line, while the small shape becomes black and the lines are thicker in the middle column.
4. **d** The small internal shape is rotated 90° clockwise and alternates colour.
5. **e** Reflective corners (note star)
6. **c** There are three of each outer shape in the grid and the shading used is the same on each row.
7. **a** [figure]

8. **b** [figure]

9. **a** [figure]

10. **d** [figure]

11. **d** [figure]

12. **e** [figure]

Section 2 Test 4 (pages 22–23)

1. **e**

2. **a**

3. **e**   (note that **b** has a flat-ended arrow)

4. **b**   (note lines are in front of white L-shape)

5. **d**

6. **d**

7. **c** Each picture has one line of symmetry.
8. **b** Each picture contains a rectangle, a curved rectangle and a hexagon with shading in the same order.
9. **d** Each picture contains six right angles.
10. **c** Each picture contains 16 sides in total.
11. **d** Each picture contains two shapes which overlap to create the same shape as them.
12. **c** Each picture contains a small oval.

Section 2 Test 5 (pages 24–25)

1. **a** First letter – number of items
Second letter – number of single-headed arrows
2. **b** First letter – type of dashed line
Second letter – number of arrow heads
3. **c** First letter – position of the small rectangle
Second letter – internal shape
4. **e** First letter – shading of central oval
Second letter – outer shape
5. **c** First letter – number of right angles
Second letter – colour
6. **a** First letter – number of rhombuses
Second letter – shading used in right-hand rhombus

7. **e** The picture rotates clockwise by an equal amount each time (135°).
8. **c** The pictures show an alternating triangle pattern, with the colour moving through the triangles from black to white.
9. **d** The picture is reflected alternately while rotating 45° clockwise.
10. **a** The picture is rotating gradually 45° clockwise.
11. **a** The angled arrow alternates direction, while the arrows increase by one in alternating directions on the correct side of the picture.
12. **e** The T-shape is rotated 45° clockwise, the arc alternates sides and the triangle moves gradually along the T.

Section 2 Test 6 (pages 26–27)

1. **e** The others contain two quadrilaterals.
2. **c** The shapes on either side of the line in the others have an equal number of sides.
3. **e** The other pictures only have two shapes.
4. **d** The others are all straight-sided shapes.
5. **d** The others all have the same size oval.
6. **a** The others are all rotations of the same shape.
7. **d** The picture is rotated 90° clockwise and then reflected in the vertical mirror line.
8. **a** The picture is rotated 180°.
9. **c** The outer shape is reflected in the horizontal mirror line, the second shape moves up out of the largest shape, the third shape reflects in the horizontal mirror line with the large shape, and the fourth shape moves into the second shape.
10. **c** The largest shape shrinks and sits in the centre of the black shape which gets bigger, and the white shape moves to the edge.
11. **d** The picture is reflected in the horizontal mirror line, the stripes swap shapes and are reflected, and black changes to white.
12. **b** The central shape elongates and goes behind, while the black shape gets bigger and turns white, and the outside shape gets smaller and turns black.

Answers

Section 3 Test 1 (pages 28–29)

1. **c** Each picture contains a rectangle and a trapezium.
2. **c** Each picture contains one thick arrow and one thin arrow pointing in opposite directions and parallel to each other, plus a black triangle and a white rectangle.
3. **d** Each is a rotation of the same picture.
4. **b** Each picture contains shapes with the same number of sides on either side of the line.
5. **c** Each picture contains 18 sides in total including the large shape.
6. **a** Each picture contains four triangles, two with the right angle bottom left and two top left; one triangle is black and is inside a quadrilateral.

If in doubt about the nets of cubes, copy them onto a piece of paper and fold them up.

7. **b**   10. **a**
8. **b**   11. **e**
9. **e**   12. **d**

Section 3 Test 2 (pages 30–31)

1. **e** The picture rotates 90° anticlockwise across the row.
2. **c** This is a repeating pattern across the row, with one pair of circles in each position in the row.
3. **a** This is a reflective pattern so that each corner uses the same dashed lines as the opposite corner and the triangle is reflected.
4. **d** The same outer shape is used across the row, the colours alternate, and the number of sides of the internal shape increases by one across the row.
5. **b** The same shape is used across the row but the colours change by moving through the shapes in the same order.
6. **e** The number of line crosses increases by one across the row, while the type of lines used across the row stays the same.

7. **a**
8. **d**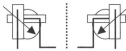
9. **d**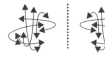
10. **b**
11. **c**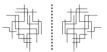
12. **b**

Section 3 Test 3 (pages 32–33)

1. **b**
2. **e**
3. **c**
4. **e**
5. **d**
6. **c**

7. **d** The others only have one black shape.
8. **a** The others all have the same three types of shading, used within the same shapes (e.g. the diamond is always black).
9. **b** The others have stripes going in two different directions.
10. **a** The others have the same number of circles as lines.
11. **b** The others all have a triangle pointing upwards.
12. **b** The others all have seven right angles.

Section 3 Test 4 (pages 34–35)

If in doubt about the nets of cubes, copy them onto a piece of paper and fold them up.

1. **c**
2. **b**
3. **d**
7. **c**
8. **e**
9. **a**
10. **e**
11. **e**
12. **c**

4. **b**
5. **d**
6. **a**

Section 3 Test 5 (pages 36–37)

1. **a** The picture is rotated 90° clockwise.
2. **d** The picture is rotated 180°, and the lines swap thickness.
3. **b** The picture is reflected in the horizontal mirror line.
4. **b** The picture is reflected in the vertical mirror line and the lines swap thickness.
5. **c** The picture is rotated by 180°.
6. **a** Each shape rotates 90° anticlockwise independently of each other and the dots change to a line.
7. **e** This is a repeating pattern except for the thick horizontal line which gradually moves down.
8. **c** The arrow rotates 45° clockwise, the square moves towards the arrow head, the circle moves away from the arrow head and the flag rotates slightly clockwise.

9. **d** The solid T-shape moves 90° clockwise.
10. **b** The line crosses reduce by one each time.
11. **e** The number of arrows and line crosses reduces by one each time.
12. **c** The arrow rotates 45° clockwise, the rectangle moves towards the arrow head and the stripes rotate 45° anticlockwise within the rectangle.

Section 3 Test 6 (pages 38–39)

1. **c** First letter – number of right angles/lines in central line
Second letter – number of sides of the small shapes
2. **a** First letter – number of arrow heads
Second letter – number of line crosses inside the outer shape
3. **d** First letter – number of sides
Second letter – shading of central shape
4. **d** First letter – number of right angles/lines in the central line
Second letter – number of rhombuses
5. **a** First letter – number of arrow heads
Second letter – type of angled line (e.g. with arrow heads/not)
6. **d** First letter – number of stars below the horizontal line
Second letter – number of stars in total
7. **e** Each picture contains a black rectangle and a white circle.
8. **c** Each picture contains 10 right angles.
9. **c** Each picture contains two circles connected to a line.
10. **b** Each picture contains only one straight non-arrowed line as well as a number of arrows.
11. **e** Each picture contains an even number of line crosses.
12. **a** Each picture contains five shapes/items.

This book of answers is a pull-out section from
Rapid Reasoning Tests: Non-verbal Reasoning 6

Published by Schofield & Sims Ltd,
Dogley Mill, Fenay Bridge, Huddersfield HD8 0NQ, UK
Telephone 01484 607080
www.schofieldandsims.co.uk

First published in 2014
Third Impression 2016

Copyright © Schofield & Sims Ltd, 2014

Author: **Rebecca Brant**
Rebecca Brant has asserted her moral right under the Copyright, Designs and Patents Act, 1988, to be identified as the author of this work.

British Library Cataloguing in Publication Data
A catalogue record for this book is available from the British Library.

Commissioned by **Carolyn Richardson Publishing Services** (www.publiserve.co.uk)

Design by **Oxford Designers & Illustrators**
Printed in India by **Multivista Global Pvt. Ltd**

ISBN 978 07217 1231 4

■ Which picture on the right can be made by combining the first two shapes?
Circle the letter.

Example

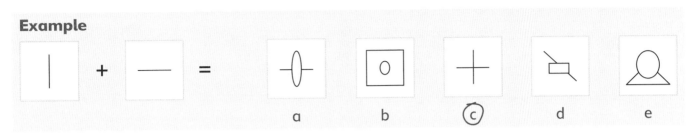

a   b   ⓒ   d   e

7.

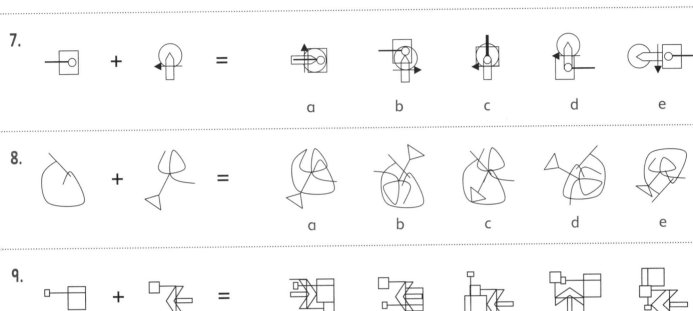

a   b   c   d   e

8.

a   b   c   d   e

9.

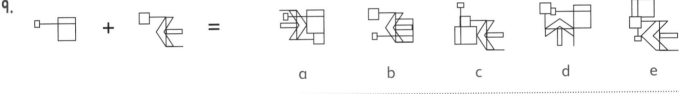

a   b   c   d   e

10.

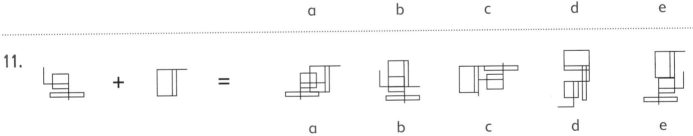

a   b   c   d   e

11.

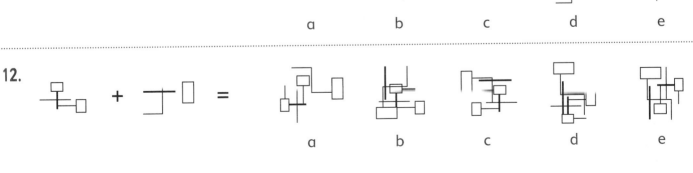

a   b   c   d   e

12.

a   b   c   d   e

End of test.

Score:		Time taken:		Target met?	

Which picture on the right is a reflection of the picture on the left? Circle the letter.

Example

 |

a   b   c   d   (e)

1. |

a   b   c   d   e

2. |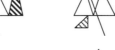

a   b   c   d   e

3. |

a   b   c   d   e

4. |

a   b   c   d   e

5. |

a   b   c   d   e

6. |

a   b   c   d   e

Now go on to the next page. ➡

■ Which picture on the right belongs to the group on the left? Circle the letter.

Example

7.

8.

9.

10.

11.

12.

End of test.

| Score: | | Time taken: | | Target met? | |

⬇
◼ What is the code of the final picture? Circle the letter.

Example

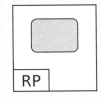

RP

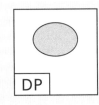

DP

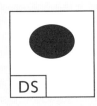

DS

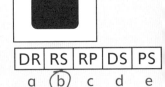

DR	RS	RP	DS	PS
a	ⓑ	c	d	e

1.

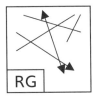

RG

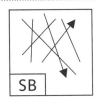

SB

RD

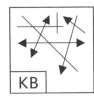

KB

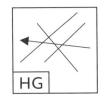

HG

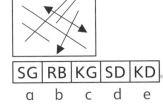

SG	RB	KG	SD	KD
a	b	c	d	e

2.

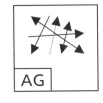

AG

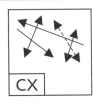

CX

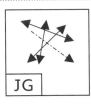

JG

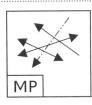

MP

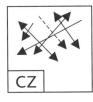

CZ

JZ	MX	AG	CP	JG
a	b	c	d	e

3.

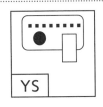

YS

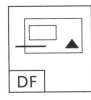

DF

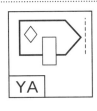

YA

ES

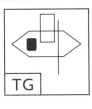

TG

TA	DS	EA	YF	TS
a	b	c	d	e

4.

RY

DF

ZS

PY

ZG

PS	ZS	DY	RG	DS
a	b	c	d	e

5.

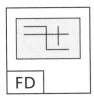

FD

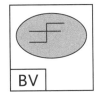

BV

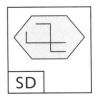

SD

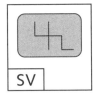

SV

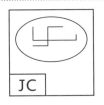

JC

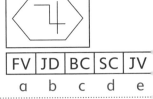

FV	JD	BC	SC	JV
a	b	c	d	e

6.

RU

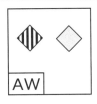

AW

NM

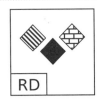

RD

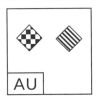

AU

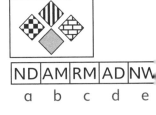

ND	AM	RM	AD	NW
a	b	c	d	e

Now go on to the next page. ➡

Which picture on the right goes in the empty space? Circle the letter.

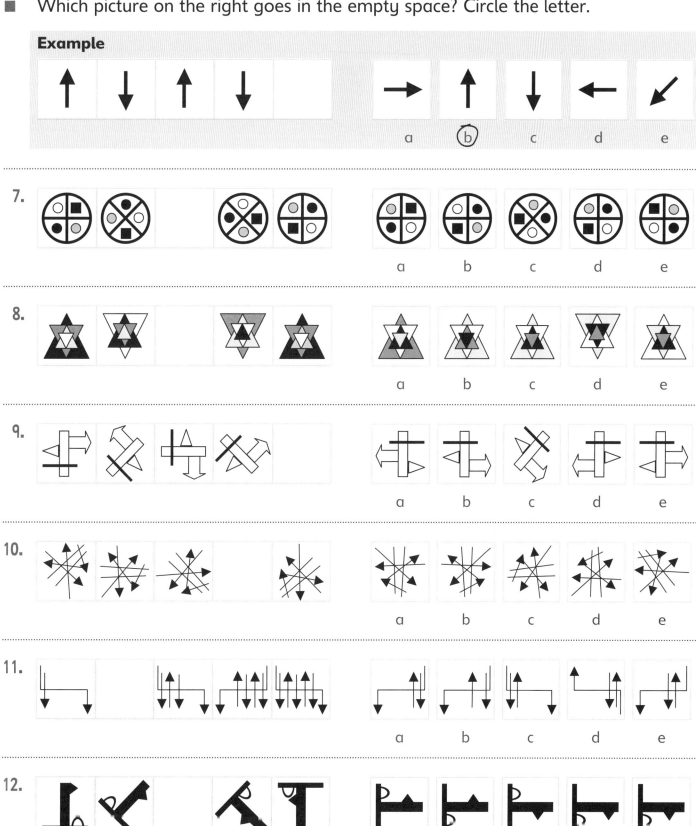

Example

a   (b)   c   d   e

7.   a   b   c   d   e

8.   a   b   c   d   e

9.   a   b   c   d   e

10.   a   b   c   d   e

11.   a   b   c   d   e

12.   a   b   c   d   e

End of test.

Score:		Time taken:		Target met?	

Which picture is the odd one out? Circle the letter.

Example

a   b   c   d   e

1.

a   b   c   d   e

2.

a   b   c   d   e

3.

a   b   c   d   e

4.

a   b   c   d   e

5.

a   b   c   d   e

6.

a   b   c   d   e

Now go on to the next page.

Which of the five pictures on the right goes with the third one to make a pair like the two on the left? Circle the letter.

Example

7.

8.

9.

10.

11.

12.

End of test.

| Score: | | Time taken: | | Target met? | |

Which picture on the right belongs to the group on the left? Circle the letter.

Example

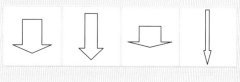

                        a   b   (c)   d   e

1.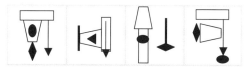

                        a   b   c   d   e

2.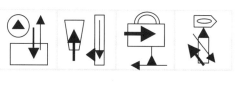

                        a   b   c   d   e

3.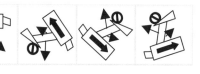

                        a   b   c   d   e

4.

                        a   b   c   d   e

5.

                        a   b   c   d   e

6.

                        a   b   c   d   e

Now go on to the next page. ➔

■ Which cube can be made exactly from the net? Circle the letter.

Example

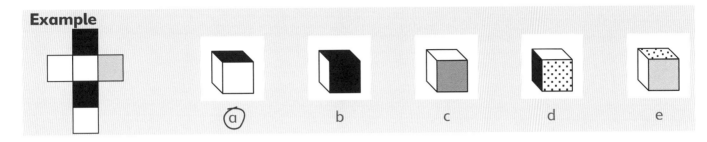

a b c d e

7.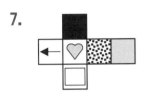

a b c d e

8.

a b c d e

9.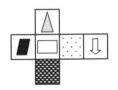

a b c d e

10.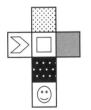

a b c d e

11.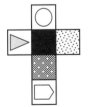

a b c d e

12.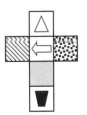

a b c d e

End of test.

Score:	Time taken:	Target met?

■ Which picture on the right best fits into the space in the grid? Circle the letter.

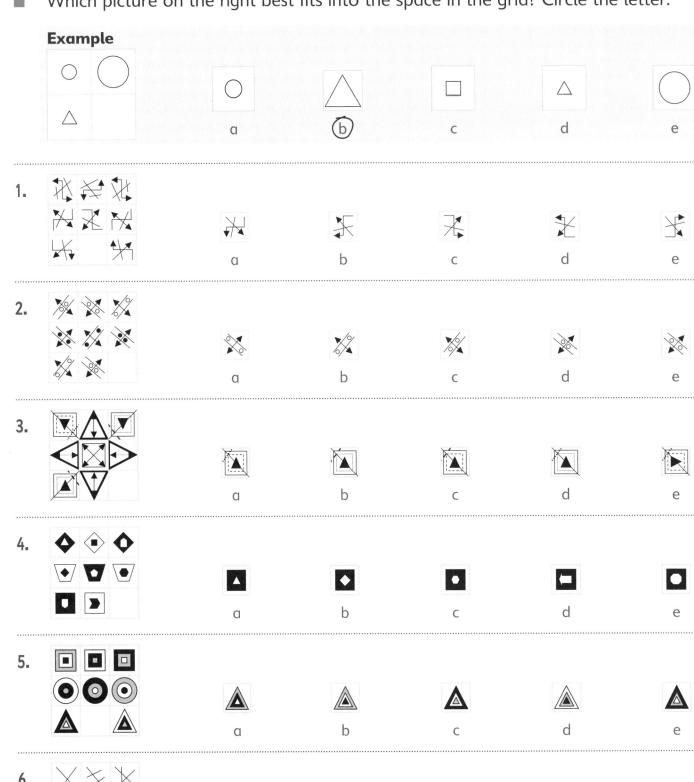

Example

a   (b)   c   d   e

1.

a   b   c   d   e

2.

a   b   c   d   e

3.

a   b   c   d   e

4.

a   b   c   d   e

5.

a   b   c   d   e

6.

a   b   c   d   e

Now go on to the next page. ➡

■ Which picture on the right is a reflection of the picture on the left? Circle the letter.

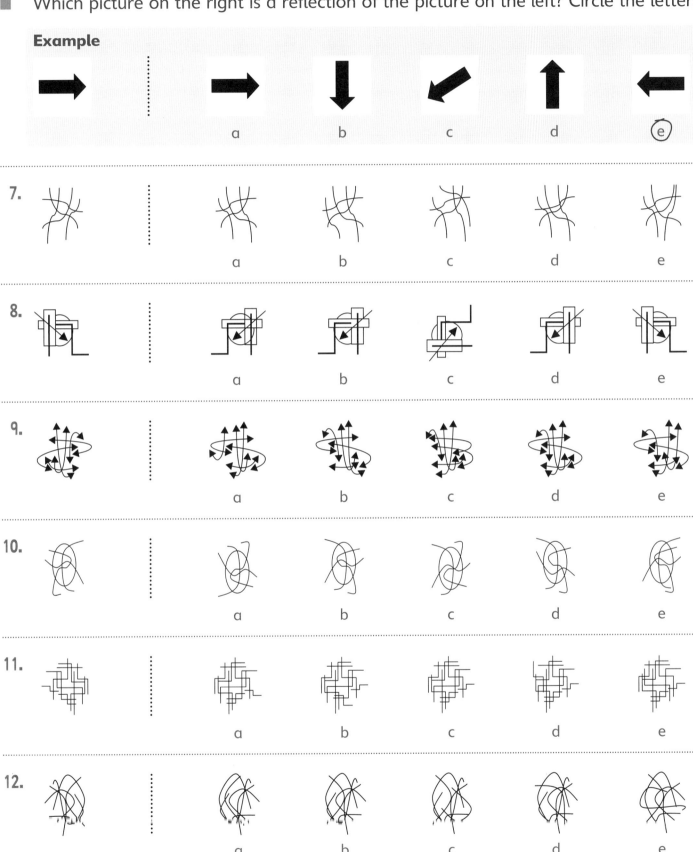

Example

a   b   c   d   (e)

7.

a   b   c   d   e

8.

a   b   c   d   e

9.

a   b   c   d   e

10.

a   b   c   d   e

11.

a   b   c   d   e

12.

a   b   c   d   e

End of test.

Score:		Time taken:		Target met?	

In which picture on the right is the picture on the left hidden? Circle the letter.

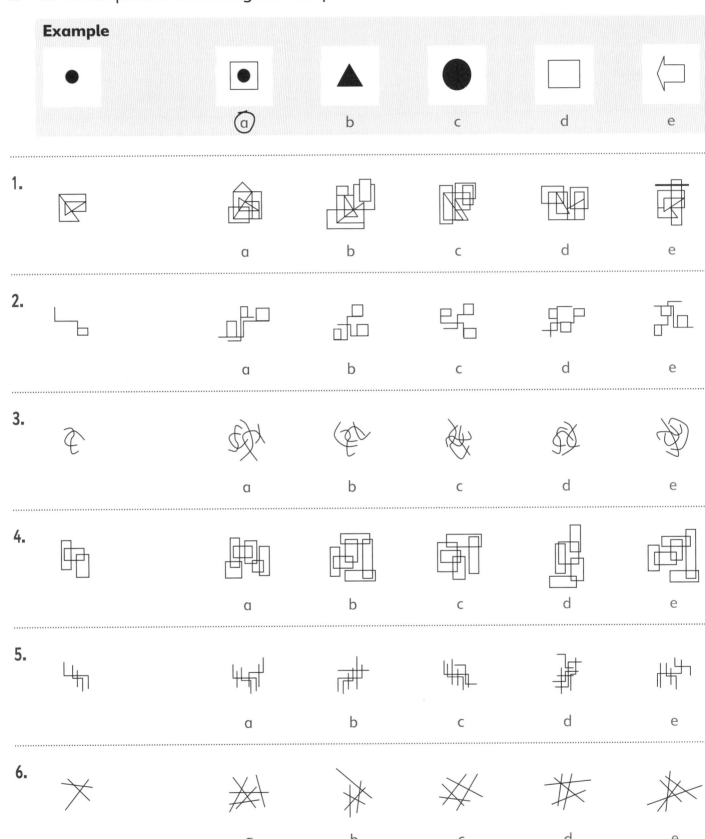

Example

| | a | b | c | d | e |

1. a b c d e

2. a b c d e

3. a b c d e

4. a b c d e

5. a b c d e

6. a b c d e

Now go on to the next page. ➡

■ Which picture is the odd one out? Circle the letter.

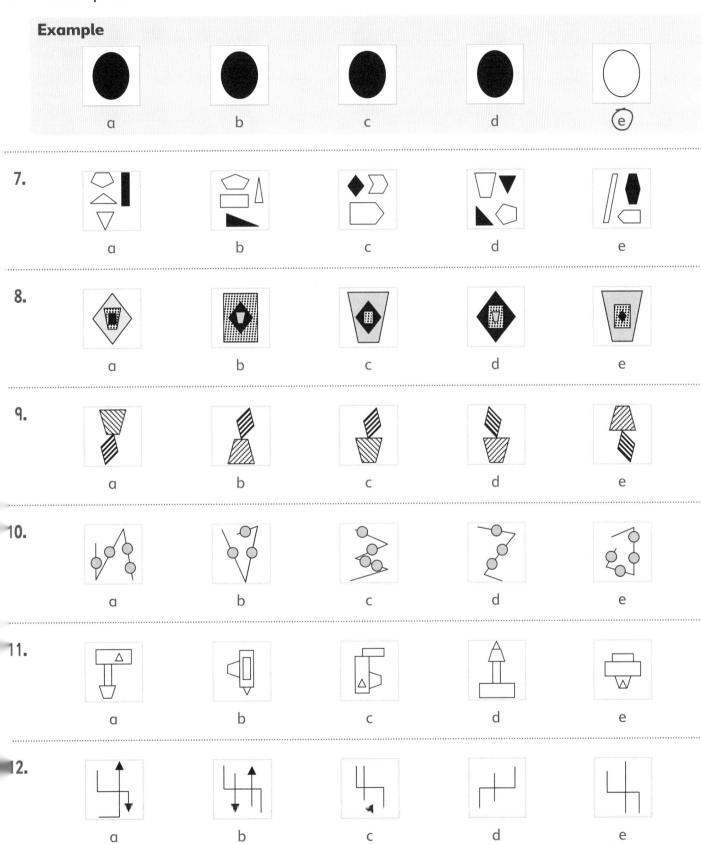

End of test.

| Score: | Time taken: | Target met? |

■ Which net can be made exactly from the cube? Circle the letter.

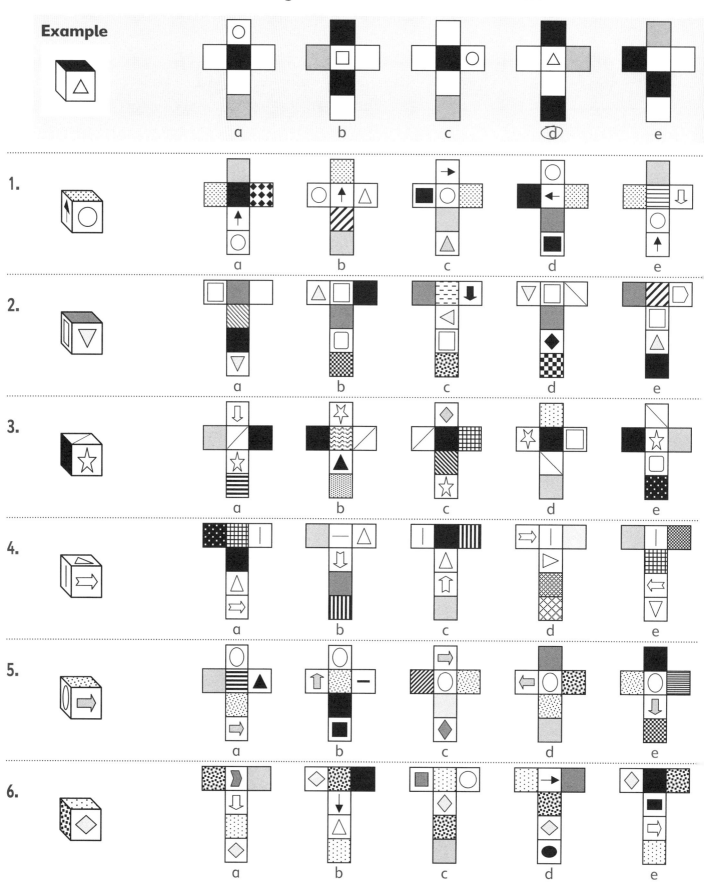

Example

a   b   c   (d)   e

1.

a   b   c   d   e

2.

a   b   c   d   e

3.

a   b   c   d   e

4.

a   b   c   d   e

5.

a   b   c   d   e

6.

a   b   c   d   e

Now go on to the next page. ➡

Which picture on the right can be made by combining the first two shapes?
Circle the letter.

Example

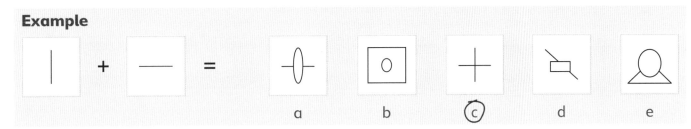

7.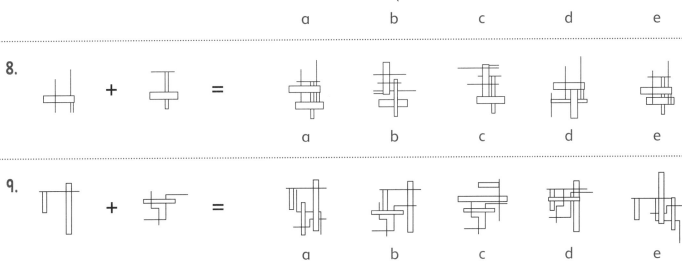

8.

9.

10.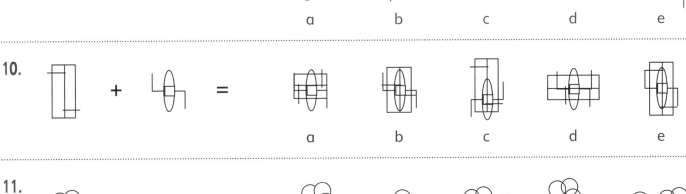

11.

12.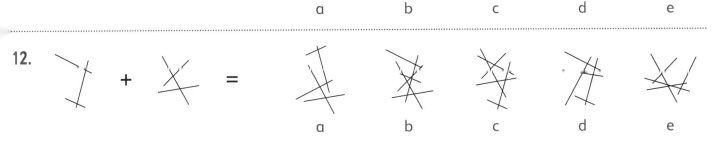

End of test.

Score:	Time taken:	Target met?

Which of the five pictures on the right goes with the third one to make a pair like the two on the left? Circle the letter.

Example

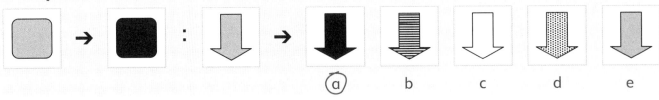

1.

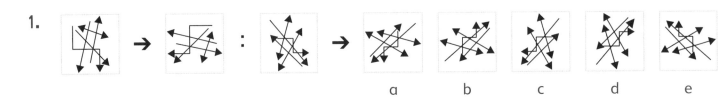

2.

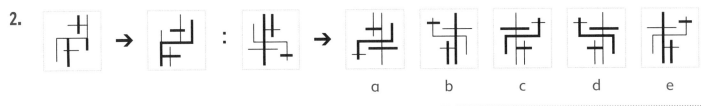

3.

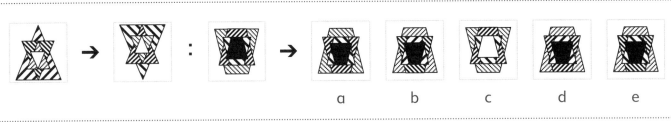

4.

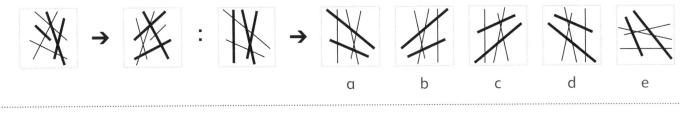

5.

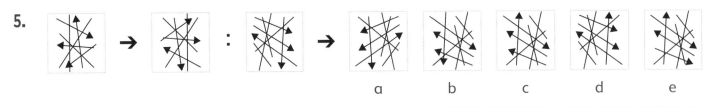

6.

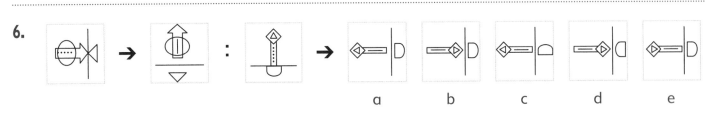

Now go on to the next page. ➡

■ Which picture on the right goes in the empty space? Circle the letter.

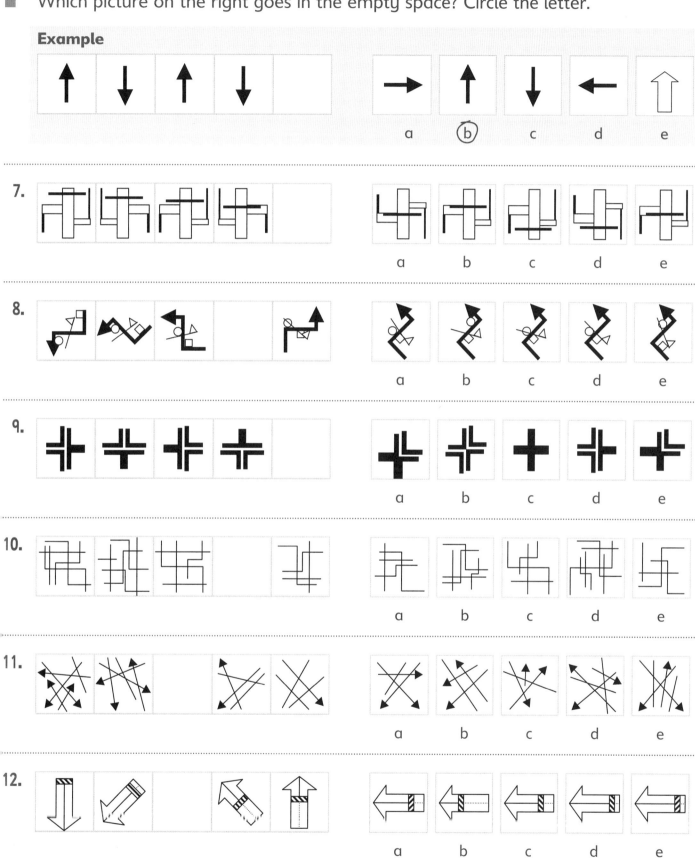

↓

What is the code of the final picture? Circle the letter.

Example

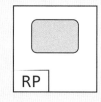 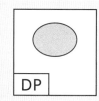 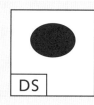 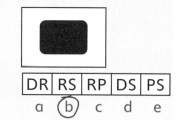

DR	RS	RP	DS	PS
a	ⓑ	c	d	e

1.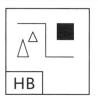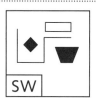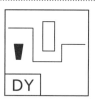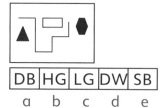

DB	HG	LG	DW	SB
a	b	c	d	e

2.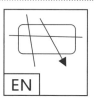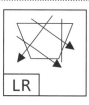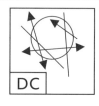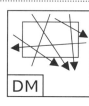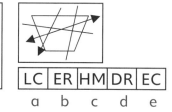

LC	ER	HM	DR	EC
a	b	c	d	e

3.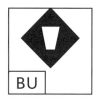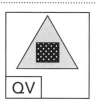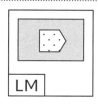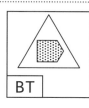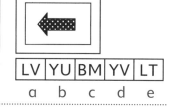

LV	YU	BM	YV	LT
a	b	c	d	e

4.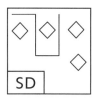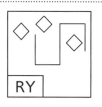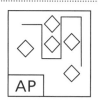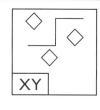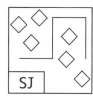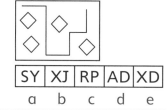

SY	XJ	RP	AD	XD
a	b	c	d	e

5.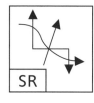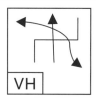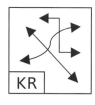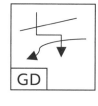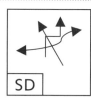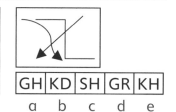

GH	KD	SH	GR	KH
a	b	c	d	e

6.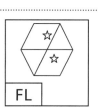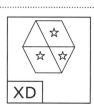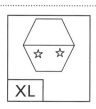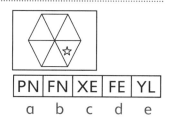

PN	FN	XE	FE	YL
a	b	c	d	e

Now go on to the next page. ➡

Which picture on the right belongs to the group on the left? Circle the letter.

Example

a   b   c   d   e

7.   a   b   c   d   e

8.   a   b   c   d   e

9.   a   b   c   d   e

0.   a   b   c   d   e

1.   a   b   c   d   e

2.   a   b   c   d   e

End of test.

Score:	Time taken:	Target met?

Schofield & Sims

the long-established educational publisher specialising in maths, English and science

Non-verbal Reasoning 6 is a collection of short, problem-solving tests based on pictures and patterns. Each timed test includes age-appropriate questions, providing opportunities for children to practise and master non-verbal reasoning skills in preparation for the 11+ and other school selection tests. This book is part of the **Rapid Reasoning Tests** series and covers the following question types: similarities and differences; missing and hidden shapes; cubes, codes and combinations.

Rapid Reasoning Tests provides short, effective, timed tests in reasoning. The series comprises six books of verbal reasoning tests and six books of non-verbal reasoning tests.

Written by experienced teachers and designed for independent use, **Rapid Reasoning Tests** has been carefully structured to provide practice of key, standard format question types. Each collection of tests has been designed for use over one year and provides one section per term in order to support regular practice.

Key features

- **Short tests** requiring few resources that are easy to fit into a busy timetable.
- A **target time** for each test encourages children to work quickly and develop the necessary exam skills for success in the 11+ and other tests.
- **Pull-out answers** in the centre of each book can be easily removed.
- **Free downloads** to support the series are available from the Schofield & Sims website.

The full series includes the following books:

Verbal Reasoning 1 978 07217 1238 3	**Non-verbal Reasoning 1** 978 07217 1226 0	**(Ages 6–7)**
Verbal Reasoning 2 978 07217 1239 0	**Non-verbal Reasoning 2** 978 07217 1227 7	**(Ages 7–8)**
Verbal Reasoning 3 978 07217 1313 7	**Non-verbal Reasoning 3** 978 07217 1228 4	**(Ages 8–9)**
Verbal Reasoning 4 978 07217 1241 3	**Non-verbal Reasoning 4** 978 07217 1229 1	**(Ages 9–10)**
Verbal Reasoning 5 978 07217 1242 0	**Non-verbal Reasoning 5** 978 07217 1230 7	**(Ages 10–11)**
Verbal Reasoning 6 978 07217 1243 7	**Non-verbal Reasoning 6** 978 07217 1231 4	**(Ages 11–12)**

MIX
From responsible sources
FSC® C110589

ISBN 978-07217-1231-4

9 780721 712314 >

ISBN 978 07217 1231 4
Key Stage 2
Age range 11–12
£3.95

For further information and to place an order visit
www.schofieldandsims.co.uk or telephone 01484 607080   **(Retail price)**